The Ka-ching Jars!

Zuhayr Fulwala

Qurate
quratebooks.com

The Ka-ching Jars!
Zuhayr Fulwala

Published in 2025

© Published by

Qurate
qurratebooks.com

Qurate Books Pvt. Ltd.
Goa 403523, India
www.quratebooks.com
Tel: 1800-210-6527, Email: info@quratebooks.com

ISBN: 978-93-58985-57-3

Acknowledgement

My heartfelt gratitude to:

My dad - my financial guide,
for believing in me.

My dear mom,
for nurturing my dreams with
warmth, wisdom, and endless care.

And my younger bro,
for being my constant companion
and confidant.

And my mentor, Ms. Deepa Bala,
who has been instrumental in
guiding me throughout this remarkable journey.

Contents

Understanding the Economy

Advanced Money Thinking

The Saving Jars

What?! You may be thinking,
Do we really need this thing?
Yes! We do indeed,
To manage every want and need!

The first 15 % goes into saving,
With a little bit of planning.
For emergencies and education,
It's a game of multiplication.

The next 15% goes into **investing**,
"So that we are not just living."
Now here's where the money grows,
Creating envy amongst friends and foes.

The next 30% are for your needs-
Everyday essentials,
Everyday deeds.

Like food, light, and a gas bill,
Life is smooth, like on a treadmill.

Now, at the end of the day,
We are all human,
We all seek some
Or the other fun.
Be it eating at a seven-star,
Or buying a lavish car.

Now the 10% is for the want -
But do not use it to flaunt!

The next 10% go for donation
For those without food, shelter,
Or education.

A little help goes a long way-
We feel good. Have a great day!

"Here am I," sneers the tax,
"If you're rich, I come in lakhs.
I come for the government,
I am everywhere-
On gifts, on bread, even on a tent.
And it's a 20 for me."

A Quick Recap!
15% to save
15% to invest
30% for daily needs
10% for your wants
10% is a donation
20% tax is a mandatory contribution.

This flow is essential-
Stay invested. Stay joyful.

Needs and Wants

"Mom, I'm thirsty. I want water."
Well, this is a need -
And of course, Essential.
"Mom, I'm thirsty. I want Coke."
Hmm...this is a want-
And of course, Optional.

Don't worry,
It's okay to have wants , too.
Just keep them rare,
Keep them few.

Wants are the ones
That make you save,
And sometimes,
Oops! Misbehave.

Needs are essentials,
Not any toy gulls.
Food, shelter, and clothes-
Not some funny jokes.
(*P.S. And definitely, not fancy egg yolks!*)

Good education
Is something to count on.
(*While reading this, try not to yawn!*)

Instant and delayed gratification

Would you sacrifice
One chocolate for two more?
Or would you rather roar,
"I can wait NO more!"
Instant gratification-
A quick want. Fun galore!

It tests your patience. That's right!
Try to control. With all your might.
But in the end, should you cave in?
Oh! Would that be a grave sin?

Choose delayed gratification instead-
I learnt this, from a book I read.

Have patience. Wait!
And strive for a bigger thing.
Does that make the bells in your mind ring?

A better guitar
Over glitter ice cream-
Here's a chase for a bigger dream.
But to know when to choose,
What's right?
I have a thought,
That sheds some light.

Why, but of course -
The stock market!
Where the bull is your prime target.

If you wait and wait,
And wait too long,
Closed will be the money gate.
Did you hear the gong?

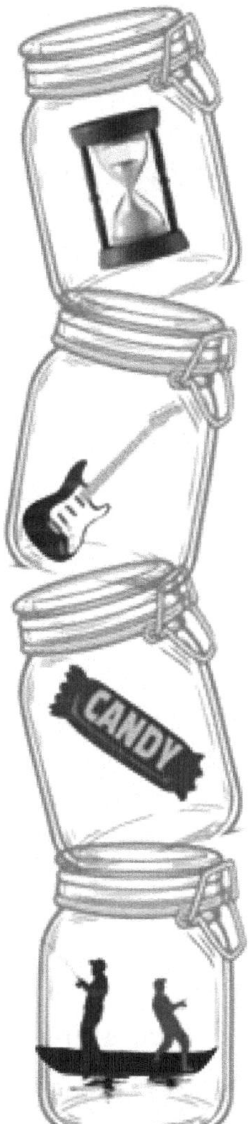

The good stocks will slip out of hand,
Dreams lost in a desert land.
Instant or Delayed?
Choose as needed.
To keep your money tree
well-seeded.

Any Time Money

Frustrating rules of banking hours
Sparked Shepherd-Barron's
Thinking powers.

He broke the rule
With an Automatic Cash Dispenser.
Aha Money! Now flows in easy measure.

While at a vending machine one day,
For a chocolate snack on his way -
Dropped a coin, a routine track,
When an idea hit him - Smack!

What if the machine
Could spit out cash?
Eureka! An Automatic Teller Machine,
A brilliant idea born in a flash.

Soon nicknamed, Any Time Money,
Just swipe your card. Begin your journey.

Payment Methods

COD - Cash on Delivery still rules
For small buys,
It's one of the tools.
A cheque is slow.
And used much less.
Write one at peace. It's no stress.

NEFT/ RTGS/ IMPS*,
Online fund transfer.
For business and bills-
It is the electronic answer,
Across rivers and hills.

Net banking,
From your website,
Moves money safely.
Quickly, day and night -
Goldilocks would smile,
"This is just right!"

Debit cards are cards
Linked to your bank account
A purchase here, a swipe there,
And "Oh Blimey!"
Take care of how you spend,
Money runs out
When the funds end.

Credit cards feel magical.
Swipe or tap to pay the usual.
Watch out!
For the Interest bite
If the date slips from sight.

While you enjoy
A month of feeling carefree,
It's a silent addiction.
Don't you see?

Google Pay, Phone Pe, and more race
To lead the (UPI) Unified Payment Interface.
Quick money transfers
Through your phone -
India's innovations
Have set the tone.

Any time you're in purchase mode,
Just scan and pay via QR code.
Now payments are
Easy-peasy lemon squeezy.
Tap or scan -
It's all so breezy.

So smooth,
Is the payment channel –
Even my dog shops online
from his kennel!

*NEFT (National Electronic Funds Transfer)
*RTGS (Real-Time Gross Settlement)
*IMPS (Immediate Payment Service)

Online vs Offline Shopping

Covid taught us a thing or two,
Online shopping pointed,
"I'm here too."
The offers are so awesome,
Hard to refuse,
Sadly, a waste. Never in use.

Online deals are on a discount,
Here, the prizes don't mount.
Wow! Right to your door delivery,
Be it books, food, or culinary.

Offline shopping stresses,
"Old is gold.
Walk into our store
See our service unfold."

May not have that good an offer,
But it's a great place for every shopper.

"Touch, try and see,
Yippee! There's no hidden fee."

There's one time I still remember,
Etched in my memory forever.
"I saw some sneakers, shiny and cool,
Clicked 'Buy Now' — oh, what a fool!"
When I tried, oh, how I cried -
"Too tight. Just not right."

So off, I went to a local store.
I tried a few and found many more.
So comfy, so neat.
Happy was I, and so were my
Wandering feet.

Know when to shop online or offline,
Research well before you sign.
Competing to win your attention,
Offline or online.
Choose your dimension.

Thrift Shopping

Look at your mom,
Bargaining with a vendor,
Searching for an offer,
Being a thrift shopper.
Always on an adventure,
Gaining experience,
Year by year!

Shopping's no longer boring,
Or mood-souring.
Compare prices store to store,
Save up twenty, look for more.
Online or offline -
Which is better?
Turn yourself into a go-getter.

Cutout coupons -
Overflowing from your hand,
Grabbing discounts.
"Oh! so grand!"

Bargain and bargain -
Is the motto of this game,
Make it your aim
To win every game.

Go on occasions or at peculiar times,
But do save one or two dimes.

Take this advice and say to yourself,
"I am good at shopping.
No wonder,
Gaining experience,
Year by Year!

Bank on Us

Dressed to the nines,
Without a doubt.
Together we set out -
To my grandpa's
Favourite hangout.

Not to a temple, nor a library,
And not the beach, you see -
A nationalized bank is what
Lights his face with glee.

He grins, "My hard-earned
Money is safe right here.
For your future-
Looks far, yet so near".

A bank statement is
Your financial report card:
Income, withdrawals,
Savings-all on record.

When money comes into the account-
Say a Salary, it's called Credit.
When money goes out of the account-
Like Expenses, it's a Debit.

You could have a
Savings Account,
Where money grows slow;
Or a Business Account
Where it's a rapid flow.

Each month,
Deposit without fail,
Compounding interest
Sets full sail.
When paying for goods
Brings on a moan -
A heavy sigh, A weary groan -
A Bank steps in with a helpful loan.

Making dreams,
Less distant. Less alone.

Insurance

Insurance is like an umbrella,
Protects you from rain.
It makes sure you are covered,
Spares you the pain!

With monthly instalments
-Tiny and manageable.
It keeps you safe,
Calm and stable.

There are various types,
Each for a season.
Some protect your health,
One for every season.

What's Life Insurance?
But a backup plan—
It protects your loved ones,
When life skips your plan.

If someone like Sam sadly bids, "Goodbye",
His family receives help—
No need to cry.

The Next is for your Car,
To cover your ride.
Any damage or disaster-
An insurance turns the tide.

Health is Wealth,
This problem is well dealt.
Should healthcare bills overflow,
An insurance may soften the blow.

Insurance is great,
Protects -
You and your mate.
It's never too late.
But don't just wait!

Tax

Why do we pay taxes?
Direct or indirect.
Where does it go?
Is there a limit
For the masses?

Why do we pay
That extra sum?
At first, it feels so Bothersome!

But, do this as a Citizen
Let's make our nation Awesome!

The government needs
Funds for every deed—
And taxes help fulfil that need.

The extra money
Goes to the State,
To build bridges, parks, schools,
And all things great.

Tax is important
For a nation's rise,
Let's not debate or criticise.

Paying taxes
Grows the economy,
We are all in this together -
Yes, you and me.

Demand and Supply

There's a simple rule in life,
Certainly, not as tough as a knife.

Here we go,
After reading, you'll know.

This rule moans, "Oh My!"
When demand is high,
And the supply is low,
Discounts - in thin air will go.

When demand is on the rise,
A product becomes twice its price.
A pizza, once priced for two,
Now it's available for one- just you.

Remember,
When the demand is high,
Supply will nearly die.
And when demand is less,
Supply is more. And in distress.

Investing

In the land of wealth,
Where dreams shine bright,
Here, coins and stocks
Take a daring flight.

We gather 'round,
With plans so grand,
To stake our claim
And take a stand.

A calculated risk,
A stocky Bear
Investing, at times,
It may not seem fair.

Investing is great,
But let me warn you,
"It's NO easy bait."

In just a day or an hour,
It can make you rich or poor.
Happy or sad,
It tests your nerves.
Just hang on!
Play smart. Don't get mad.

Investing is more of a game,
The more you practice, the closer you aim.
Analyse the lines. Study the signs.
Decide what you want to do.
Buy or sell - it's up to you.

With this, I hate to say, "Bye",
Next time you're rich,
Should you pass by
Just give a wave, or say "Hi!"

Bulls Vs Bears

Bulls are heroes,
People say, "Bulls are just great."
But are they? Really?
Is it true? Let's calculate.

In investing,
Bulls are the ones who see you rise
Mood is happy. Stocks take flight.
With the Bulls around,
Budgets, too, feel awfully light.

Oh Bears!
Well, everybody hates them.
Wait. Did I hear someone say -
"I lost my 10000 yen today?"

Bears are just the opposite of bulls,
Hold on tight!
Brace for the falls and the pulls.
They bring stocks crashing down.
Some fall. Some fear. Some frown.

But "Thank you, Bear!"
Because without you, there's no Bull.
After every fall comes a rise -
"The golden rule", said the wise.

"Bear oh Bear,
I feel pity for you, I surely do!
Bull. Oh Bull!
I feel proud when I am with you."

When the Bull thrusts his horns
The markets triumph.
Should the bear swipe its paws,
The markets slump.

I respect both the Bull and the Bear,
Together, they hold the market. Fair!

"We can never unite", they snarl at me.
"Come on, Bear - Don't just glare at me."

Shares and Stocks

Shares are bites of a tasty cake,
Grab a slice - for heaven's sake.
If the company grows, your shares will. Yahoo!
But if it sinks, well, Boo-Hoo!

Stocks - you may have heard of them,
If you haven't,
Hear it now.
Delve deeper,
And you'll exclaim,
"Oh. Wow!"

It's a part of a company, a tiny block,
A share is one unit of a stock.
But stay steady-
Don't get a shock!

When you buy a stock,
You own one share.
Hold your breath -
Invest with care.
If the stock goes up,
Give yourself a treat!
Continue the good work,
Do not cheat.

Before you buy,
Research well,
If it flops,
Please don't yell.
Remember,
Patience is the key.
With this motto,
You'll succeed.
This, I guarantee.

Barter to Bitcoins

In medieval times,
There weren't any dimes.
So sad -
But people weren't mad.

They started the exchange of goods,
Like trading goats for neighbouring goods.
You guessed it right.
Tedious though,
They tried with all their might.
Some traders found this unfair,
And raised their hands in despair.

Came up with something not so bright,
Better than barter - an idea, a new light.
Rolled in copper, silver, shells, and gold,
However, these were hard to mould.
Copper for gold was no good trade.
Tell you what. "They weren't greatly made."

They came up with something new.
Gold coins with a certain value.
This worked well for a while,
But too heavy to tug a mile.

In came China,
With something lighter,
Something easier,
And truly mightier.
The paper prints, they claimed,
A money currency - globally famed.

But where to keep the money?
On a day not so sunny?
Ah yes! It was the bank,
Cash in a big old tank.
A little cheesy!

They introduced mobile wallets
-How great!
People cheered, "Wow Mate!"
With a click of a button, money flew -
The best idea anyone knew!
But they had a certain limit,
Soon, the hype of it
Slipped down bit by bit.

Then came credit and debit cards,
No need for safe or security guards.

Surged in a tidal wave of cryptocurrency,
As smooth as honey - digital money.

No need to step out on a rainy day.
Investing or trading is your way.

In 2050, who knows
What tech will bring?
More Bitcoins or a Magical ring?
Just one tap and a ding!
You will be left cheering!

Remember,
Money evolves. Money grows.
Goats, rupees, coins, or rings -
Nobody knows.

So, let's be prepared
For evolutions to come.
Okay,
Now back to my math sums!

Money Affirmations

I am smart with my money.

I make good choices when I spend.

I am happy to save for things I care about.

I can earn money by using my talents.

I make my goals possible by saving money.

I believe I can build a bright and rich future.

I am grateful for all the things I have.

I invest in learning to strengthen my future.